THE ADVENTURES OF CARRY KINDNESS

Text and Illustrations Copyright © 2021 by Nancy Raciti

All rights reserved. No part of this publication may be reproduced, stored in a retrieval system, or transmitted in any form or by any means – for example, electronic, photocopy, recording – without the prior written permission of the publisher.

Carry Kindness® is a registered trademark of Grace & Kind, LLC
The Carry Kindness image is Copyright 2017 by Grace & Kind, LLC

Written by Nancy Raciti
Illustration & Graphic Design by Cabala Animation, LLC, cabalastudio.com

Published by Grace & Kind, LLC
P.O. Box 345, Boise, ID 83701
www.graceandkind.com

ISBN: 978-1-7359224-0-9 (hardback)
ISBN: 978-1-7359224-1-6 (paperback)
ISBN: 978-1-7359224-2-3 (ebook)

Library of Congress Control Number: 2020919644

GRACE & KIND
BOISE, IDAHO

This book is dedicated to my mama, Barbara Currell.
Thank you for introducing me to the King of Kindness, Jesus.

*Eternal gratitude to
Mrs. Abby Fremouw
for the 1st launch of Carry*

★ ★ ★

*Thanks to the amazing beta
readers from
Sorensen Magnet School
Coeur d' Alene, Idaho
2019-2020*

Levin, Oliver, Raddek, Ben, Logan, Tyler, Heidi, Sam, Camden, Margret, Jeanilly, Marlys, Rhena, Zavi, Owen, Eloise, Peppy, Orion, Magnus, Noah, Frankie, Austen, Molly, Fiona, Sawyer, Elsa, Gretchen, Mrs. Holly Weymouth, Quinley, Colin, Lillian, Lilo, Aria, Mia, Loretta, Tia, Camden, Bella, Harlan, Alice, Max, Elle, Everett, Nik, Charlie, Joelle, Mitch, Bentlee, Nora, Coltyn, Lilli, Marly, Summer, Skylar

The Adventures of Carry Kindness

NANCY RACITI

GRACE & KIND
BOISE, IDAHO

Lily is a sweet, young girl in Idaho.

She lives with her family on a street lined with trees and not too far from the river that flows through town.

Lily's very favorite thing to do is play at the park with her friends, Eva and Alex. The park where they play is vast and green and has a playground on top of a tall hill.

They love to climb to the top of the hill and draw pictures. After they finish their artwork, they all roll down the big hill to the soft patches of flowers at the bottom. Then they hold hands and run back up the hill, just to roll down again.

One day, as Lily, Eva, and Alex climbed toward the top of their favorite hill, Lily saw a new kid she hadn't seen before.

The little boy was sitting on the swing, all alone. His head hung low, and his toes dragged against the wood chips beneath him.

Lily wasn't sure what to do. She didn't know that boy. She had never seen him before.

Just then, Eva spoke up. "That's Matt. My brother and I saw him yesterday. He was alone then too. He's not very friendly. We don't play with him."

Eva's comment had Lily wondering if Matt really liked being alone.

Eva, Lily, and Alex ran back up the hill.

When they arrived at the hilltop, Alex laid out a blanket. Eva shared her bucket of crayons. Lily handed them each a piece of paper.

"I'm drawing that tree over there!" Alex exclaimed.

"I'm drawing the birds and the fluffy white clouds," Eva remarked.

Lily, on the other hand, could not stop thinking about the new boy, Matt. He looked so sad. Lily colored quickly.

She drew a girl with a big smile.

"What did you draw?" Alex asked Lily.

"A picture for that boy over there," she began. "He probably just needs some kindness. Maybe he's not very friendly because he doesn't know us yet."

Suddenly, Lily knew just what to do!

"Come on, everyone! Let's roll down the hill. I'll meet you at the bottom. I've got an idea!" she shouted.

Lily, Eva, and Alex rolled down the grassy hill. Everyone giggled as they landed in the flower patch.

Lily stood and said, "Let's pick some flowers to give to that new kid, Matt! Maybe if we say hi and ask if he wants to play, he can be our friend."

"He's not very friendly," Eva reminded Lily.

"Maybe he's just shy," suggested Alex.

"Let's give it a try!" agreed Eva.

All three children picked flowers in the field until they had put together a beautiful bouquet.

"Let's invite Matt to roll with us!" Lily suggested as she beamed with excitement.

Lily, Alex, and Eva walked over to Matt.

"Hi," Lily started. "You must be Matt. I'm Lily. This is Alex and Eva. I drew you this picture."

Eva handed him the bouquet. "We picked these flowers for you!"

"Thanks," Matt mumbled as he took the picture from Lily and the flowers from Eva.

"Would you like to play with us?" Lily asked.

Matt held the bouquet and looked down. Glancing up, he saw Alex, Eva, and Lily smiling at him. He looked again at the picture and then at the flowers.

Matt's face broke into a big smile.

"Yes, I want to play with you guys!" he answered happily.

Together, Matt, Lily, Eva, and Alex rolled down the hill, played hide-and-seek, and lost themselves in a game of tag until the sun began to set.

One by one, the friends were called home for dinner. Lily and Matt walked together across the field.

"Thank you for being so kind to me," Matt said softly. "I just moved here. I've been hoping to find a friend."

Lily smiled. "I'm glad we're friends! And I hope when you look at the drawing I gave you, you will remember to carry kindness with you. I can't wait to play again!" she giggled.

At home, around the dinner table, Lily's mom asked about her day at the park. "Did you have fun with your friends?"

Lily smiled. "I did! We made a new friend today—just by being kind!"

Matt took his picture and flowers home. In his room, he looked at the drawing that Lily had given him. The smile on the girl's face brought a smile to his face as he thought of the kindness of his new friends.

I know, he thought. *I'll call her Carry. Carry Kindness.*

Matt folded the drawing of Carry Kindness and tucked it safely into his backpack.

Later that evening, Matt called his friend in North Dakota, where he used to live.

"Hi, Sarah!" Matt greeted her with excitement.

"Hello, Matt," she replied. Matt could hear the sadness in her voice. "I had a bad day today. I used to have you to play with, but today I was alone on the playground, and the other kids laughed at me," she confided.

Sarah's confession saddened Matt. He knew how it felt to be alone.

Matt knew just what to do. "Sarah, I'm going to send you a letter, okay?"

Sarah's voice perked up. "That would help. Thanks, Matt. You're a good friend."

When Sarah received her letter, she opened the envelope to find a brightly colored picture of a smiling girl.

The letter read:

<blockquote>

This is Carry Kindness.

You can take her with you to
remind you that kindness
will always make things better.

I made some more Carrys
for you to color and
share with others.

Carry Kindness helped me
make new friends here.
She'll help you too.

Miss you lots!

-Matt

</blockquote>

Sarah colored each one of the Carrys Matt had sent her and gave them out on the playground during recess.

After recess, a curious teacher, Mr. Henderson, stopped her. He said, "Sarah, what is this you've been handing out?"

"Carry Kindness!" Sarah exclaimed. "She reminds everyone to be kind wherever they go. She came all the way from Idaho!"

"What a wonderful idea!" Mr. Henderson replied. "Hey, do you think I could have one of those Carrys? I have a friend in Illinois who could use an unexpected smile."

Sarah couldn't believe the teacher wanted one too, and she kindly gave him her last one.

Mr. Henderson sent a letter, some chocolates, and Carry Kindness to his friend, Mrs. Jenkins, all the way in Chicago.

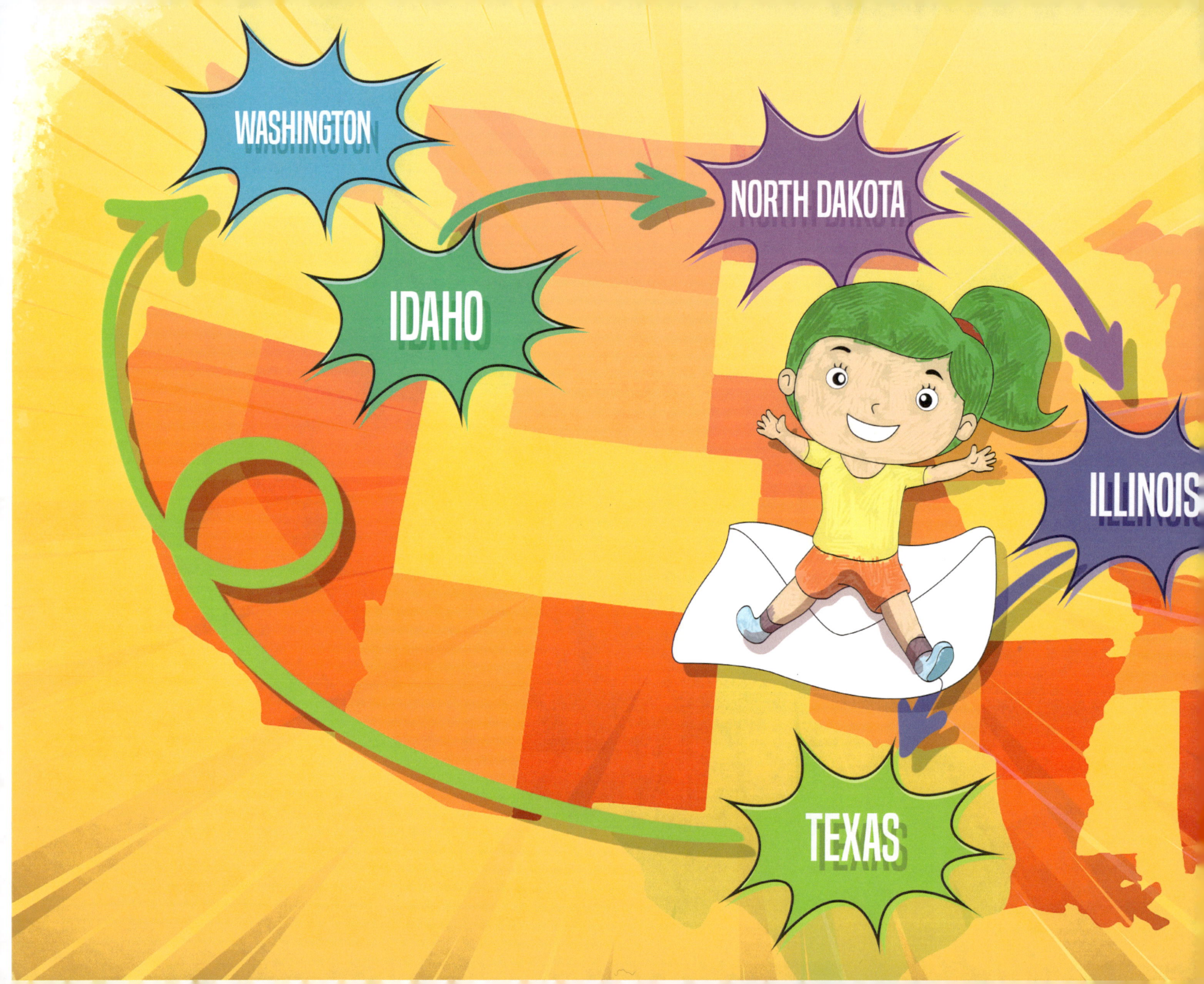

Mrs. Jenkins in Chicago loved Carry Kindness and the sweet treats so much that she sent Carry and a pretty drawing to her great-nephews in Texas.

Her great-nephews sent Carry and a fun book from Texas to their cousins in Washington.

Those cousins cleaned their rooms without being asked and then sent Carry to their friend's school in India.

Back in Idaho, Matt found himself alone at the park again. Since no one was there to play with him, he decided to walk home. Before heading in the house, he opened the mailbox to bring in the mail.

As he reached in, a yellow envelope caught his eye. He looked and was happily surprised to see it was a letter for him!

When he opened the envelope, his smile began to grow as he saw a brightly colored picture of Carry Kindness smiling back at him.

Help Carry Kindness on her mission to carry kindness all over the world!

Did you know that one little act of kindness can make someone's day brighter?
And, studies show that doing an act of kindness will make you happier too!

Let's get started!

Color the picture of Carry found in this book.
While you're coloring, think about some acts of kindness
you and Carry can do together.

Here are a few ideas to get you started:

★ Fill out the postcard in the back of this
book and mail it to someone to brighten their day.

★ Tell someone a joke and enjoy the laughter.

★ Help someone with a chore—without being asked.

You can even send her to a friend so they can do an act of kindness.
It's fun to see where your Carry —and kindnesses—travel!

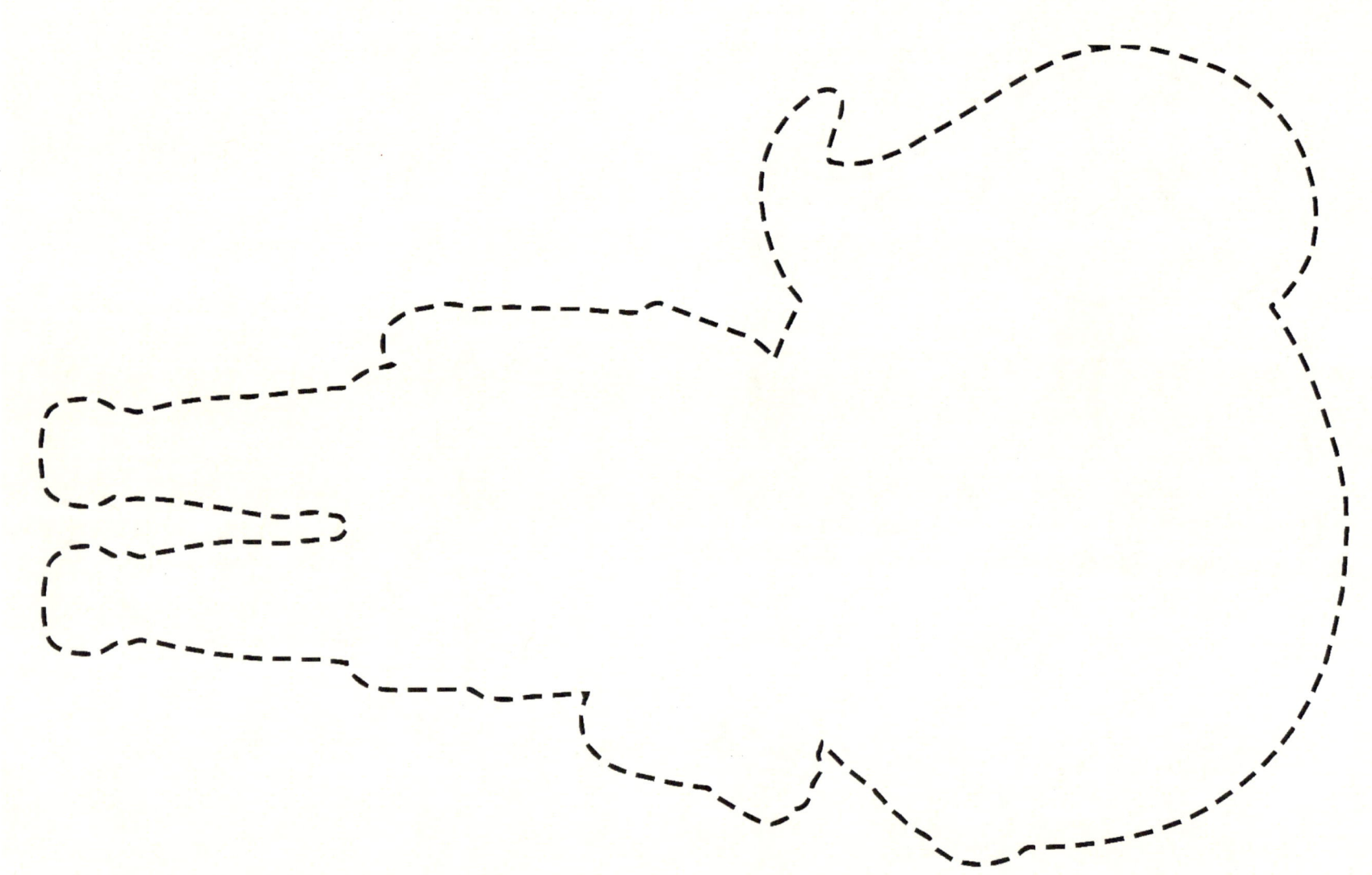

CPSIA information can be obtained
at www.ICGtesting.com
Printed in the USA
BVRC101654100222
628587BV00003B/61